THE BEGINNING IS NEAR

EVENFALL

Copyright © 2023 by Evenfall

All rights reserved. No part of this publication may be reproduced, distributed, or transmitted in any form or by any means, including photocopying, recording, or other electronic or mechanical methods, without the prior written permission of the publisher, except in the case of brief quotations embodied in critical reviews and certain other noncommercial uses permitted by copyright law.

The Poetics Publishing is an imprint of The Poetics GmbH - a software and publishing company based in Zug, Switzerland.

For inquiries contact: evenfall@thepoetics.eu

ISBN 978-3-03971-008-9 Paperback
ISBN 978-3-03971-009-6 Hardback
ISBN 978-3-03971-010-2 E-book

The Poetics GmbH
Hasenbüelweg 34
6300 Zug – Switzerland

For the dreamers who create their own story.

THE BEGINNING IS NEAR

She smiled and the universe
turned into a happier place.

THE BEGINNING IS NEAR

Far from the skies,
are the heavens
that melt in a love
deeper than the oceans.
A home for dreamers,
for us, the perfect lovers.
A paradise in a universe
we have been searching for.

Love is easy with the right one — Love gives you the strength to live moments with peace and with the right one it's difficult to imagine your life without them. There is always a desire to walk through every path, hand in hand. Maybe love is something that speaks through the eyes and is felt by the soul.

Under a sea of thousand stars,
I drowned in your eyes anyway.

She — She is one of those filled with adventure. A woman of dreams, the one who gets lost in those skies that you keep staring at on a breezy gentle evening. She was meant to fly, with her heart always choosing to see the light. She's a healer to the heart, a hope for the universe.

THE BEGINNING IS NEAR

Every single time I look into your eyes
I fall in love a little more
than once with you.

THE BEGINNING IS NEAR

> She has a fire in her,
> turning heaven into hell.

THE BEGINNING IS NEAR

I started loving you
from the shadows
after you warned me
of the dying light within you.

I have surfed too many waves
but in you, I drowned myself.

THE BEGINNING IS NEAR

We went
through it all
just to be
strangers again.

THE BEGINNING IS NEAR

You gifted me scars and a heart
that breaks a little more every day.

Loss — Sometimes you try your best and fight hard for someone only to realise that they weren't meant to be yours. You hold onto your past and choose to take responsibility for all the hurt, while they have moved on in life. But soon enough you should know that you've been too hard on yourself, and it's time for you to let go of everything that weighs you down, of everything that connects you to the memories of pain and suffering. Soon enough you should know that life is more than grieving the loss of a person you thought would be yours.

Some hearts
aren't blessed to beat together.

The beauty of healing — One of the most painful aspects of a heartbreak is that it completely defies the way you've been used to do things. Sometimes it seems like you're entirely powerless and that you'll never be able to move on from the pain and discomfort. Everyone recovers from sadness at a different pace. You may also need more time to heal from some relationships than you do from others, especially the ones that have lasted longer or have been more valuable to you in some way. It is critical to accept the end of your relationship and all the emotional stress of moving on from your grief that comes with it. The truth is that, like everything else in life, melancholy does not linger indefinitely. You will experience brighter days again, as well as happiness and affection in your immediate vicinity. There's a good chance that you have sacrificed a bit of yourself in the relationship, so now is your opportunity to locate yourself once more. The only thing left to do is to rediscover the personal qualities that made you unique; all that remains is for you to recreate the feeling of peace, because pain is followed by the beauty of healing.

Some goodbyes haunt you forever.

Ever since you left
I've forgotten the taste of love.

Love isn't enough — The bitter truth is that you cannot make them stay by loving them harder. Some memories will ache your soul, hoping they would have lasted forever. Don't let your loneliness sink and drown you. The storm within you will only calm down when you learn to let go, for you can miss them and still not want them back. It is okay to grieve the loss of someone who was an important part in your life and who once made you smile, but don't let your mind trick you into re-entering a toxic cycle with them. Most of the times, when it all ends, that is the moment you realise your worth. The ending makes way for a better beginning.

THE BEGINNING IS NEAR

There is a gloom
in the clouds with no sun,
it seems as though
every day is here
to remind me
of my aching
without you.

Failure — Dealing with failure usually requires self-motivation, will, and encouragement. Everyone fails at some point in their lives. The only difference is that some individuals choose to get up and go ahead while others opt to remain seated. When you've experienced a setback, it's tempting to believe that you'll constantly fail in this area of your life. When a failure occurs, most individuals are harsh on themselves. There is an instant feeling of sadness, sorrow, and even loss. In the glare of someone else's excellence, failure may seem much more terrible. But remember, these challenges always enable us to grow and become more resilient. We will be unable to deal with comparable circumstances in the future if we choose to ignore and flee rather than deal with them. It is completely up to us how we perceive it and how we look at it. Too often, everyone focuses on the bad things that happen when things go wrong. When terrified of failure, they stop trying altogether but you must have faith in yourself that you will be able to make it work in the end. You must be able to overcome the most severe hurdles and setbacks while allowing the dread of failure not to overwhelm you.

THE BEGINNING IS NEAR

Love is as easy as breathing
but when you're around,
my heart sinks as deep
as the bottom of a sea.

Actions over words — When someone betrays your confidence, it might be difficult to trust them again since you already feel let down. While words may be dishonest, vibes and actions never are. When someone disrespects you, try to be aware of their behaviour and ask yourself whether they are worth fighting for. Why would you cry over someone who doesn't appreciate your feelings, or think about someone who makes you feel horrible about yourself? If they make no effort, it is more likely that they do not feel the same way about you. It is crucial that you understand when and where to contribute and how much of yourself to give during every stage of your life. Do not hang on when respect is no longer being shown to you. You become more mature in your perspective on life as a result of all these small, self-directed actions and thoughts, and you gain a better understanding of how to approach various life circumstances.

They leave you
hurt and broken,
but you still call it love?

Wrong people — No matter who you are or what you have, no one has the right to make you feel bad about yourself. The right person will never make you feel unworthy. They will never make you feel like you're not good enough, or like you don't matter. They will always see the best in you and remind you why you're worth spending time with. Always remember this.

THE BEGINNING IS NEAR

The thought of
holding on to a love
that felt like yours
destroyed me
anyway.

You deserve better — I understand how sensitive you are because of the pain they have given you. You keep breaking down, thinking about people from your past, even though they've most likely moved on. I understand how you must be feeling deep inside, having spent so much of yourself on them, dreaming of a future with them in it. It's unbelievable how quickly someone's sentiments can change, and now when you're trapped behind, in denial, blaming yourself for all the agony, all I can say is that some hearts aren't blessed to beat together. Accept what has happened; there is nothing you can do about it. It may appear tough at first but remove yourself from anything that connects you to them. Your soul always deserves the best. Take your time healing, but don't keep looking for love in the midst of your pain. Healing might be difficult, but it always improves with time. The wounds may linger, but you're paving the way for better things in life by prioritising yourself before everyone else.

Some songs hurt you but in a different way,
bringing back the bitter-sweet memories.

Feeling deeply — We all have those moments where we don't feel complete, letting time run away. We all have days when we want to escape from feeling some emotions, those that numb a part of us. We have a lot of expectations from our younger selves. And for some reasons, not everything we try will end up working out, and that's okay. You still have the time to figure it out, what is right and what is wrong. And what's meant for you, will always find you. Sometimes you get so used to facing rejections, that what you fail to notice is that you're still trying, and that's what strong people do. Keep doing, keep trying. Life is beautiful, and it's okay to feel these emotions deeply, all of them.

When hearts break
they can never go back
to being the same again,
for now I'm too broken
to be loved by you
ever again.

Emptiness — Some days affect you in a different way, especially at night. When the lights go out and it grows darker, the heart aches a bit more. It's as if you're weighing the guilt, regret, and suffering all at once, hoping for things to improve and make it easier for you to breathe. You keep dwelling on the things that did not go your way, with the thought of emptiness filling the spaces in your heart. When you're feeling down or empty, remember that it's good to take your time and walk alone until you feel like yourself again. There will be hard moments, and you will be forced to be strong, which is sometimes the only way to deal with them. But most importantly, they will teach you to value every moment that you live and have.

THE BEGINNING IS NEAR

My heart feels like
it's about to break
for all the things
it tried to become
in the memory
of loving you.

Every night
I become less of myself
and more of a person
I can't recognize any longer.

Anxiety — I know you have been struggling with anxiety and are becoming exhausted. You've been pushing yourself into the dark in hopes of seeing some light. I understand how difficult it may be when your inner voices are screaming at you, fighting alone, with no one to listen to you. The truth is that you are your own light in the darkness. You're sensitive, yet you're also powerful enough to achieve anything in life, even if you can't see your potential. Bad days allow your greatest strengths to shine through, and the suffering allows for growth and healing.

I carry the whole universe in me
but on some nights
you'll find me crumble
and break into two.
Often I'm my own enemy.

Burden — What's not yours is not for you to carry. It's difficult but there's nothing you can do. You have to accept that some things are not meant to be and nothing will change that. Find a way to let go of these things and focus on those that are here and that you do have. Moving on is the only way to be free and to find happiness again, to find yourself again.

THE BEGINNING IS NEAR

Don't break your heart trying to fix someone.

Pain — I understand how tough it is to put your faith in someone, especially when so far you've only been hurt in return. I know how it feels to give someone your whole self and have them shatter it into two halves. It feels as if you've lost a piece of yourself. But all the battles you fight every day to bring yourself closer to happiness will make sense one day. As long as you don't lose faith in the universe's power, your wings will be capable of carrying you through, and every setback will shape you into a better version of yourself. It's inspiring to see how you can carry so much pain and still rise above it all.

THE BEGINNING IS NEAR

We live and breathe
on words we might never
have the courage to say.
Maybe this is why
pain continues to win.

Realisations — When we encounter anything in life that we desire, we may get too attached to it out of fear of losing it completely. The most difficult but ultimately most essential thing to do at such times is to recognize that life is always trying to teach you something and you have to trust its flow. It isn't easy to drop the feeling or the situation that has made a home within you, but you have to let go of what does not serve you. Things we have no control over may cause our minds to become focused on them, so it is beneficial to identify what we can change and what we cannot, and then to completely let go and trust that life will develop precisely as it should. We spend so much of our lives growing attachments to things that our lives become overloaded with petty things which, in the end, don't matter to us at all anymore.

Don't let your loneliness
invite you into a toxic cycle.

Let go of what hurts you,
love more of what heals you.

Solitude — Sometimes it can be mentally exhausting when interacting with people drains your energy. While being alone provides the ideal time for self-reflection, you have more time to heal from your own past problems, as well as rectify yourself and grow from it. When we interpret it negatively, we experience loneliness. But resting is not a sign of failure as long as you decide where you're going. Take the time and consider how things fit into your life and if it's worthwhile to give your all to something that doesn't fulfill your full potential.

THE BEGINNING IS NEAR

I was too whole
to feel empty
before I met you.

Moving on — Life can be unpredictable. It doesn't matter what it was like five years ago; you can't always have the people you wished to spend the rest of your life with. As the days pass, your heart begins to get chilly. You may feel dissatisfied or agitated for no reason at times. All we can do is wait and hope that the awful things will eventually end or at least slow down. But, in the end, we must all recognise that both time and pain are transient. We just lose ourselves when we think about the ones who have hurt us. You have the life you were given, and it's okay to let go of the things that are holding you back. That's when you begin living your life here and learning to appreciate yourself. There will be no turning back to unfortunate moments in the past. When you replace them with yourself, the healing will come quickly.

Pain is often a blessing
to show that you deserve better.

Know your worth — You will meet individuals who do not appreciate what you do, who do not return your efforts, and who do not attempt to create a good connection with you. It's alright to move on if you're unable to cope in a scenario where you're treated poorly. You will have to disappoint some people along the journey and set certain limits that may be difficult for you to do, but it is necessary to do so when there are people who don't allow you any breathing space. There are so many reasons to keep going, don't lose it for all the wrong ones.

THE BEGINNING IS NEAR

When it hurts, let go.
Remember what you deserve.

Pain changes people — Some wounds cut so deeply to help you see how much power you have within you. Pain allows you to flourish, drives you to seek light in the shadows, and is often the only path to recovery.

Reality — It is important to let go of what pulls you down deep inside your heart. When breathing becomes a reminder of how tough it is to find calm in the midst of chaos and in the evenings when emptiness consumes you, you cling to memories from your past. The reality is, your heart will not always feel this heavy. The moment you realise you've been too hard on yourself by taking on guilt and burdens that aren't yours, it will find a reason to beat and a purpose to breathe.

You only fly when you set yourself free.

Walking alone — You will ultimately be rewarded with a more optimistic view of life when you experience and overcome challenging conditions. You'll start to value the small things that really matter, and you'll feel gratitude welling up within you. Don't be afraid to walk through your difficult moments alone since you're meant to shine as a result of them.

You learn more of yourself

as you lose someone.

Self-awareness — It is a quick route to anxiety and isolation if you focus your sense of worthiness on what others think of you or what they think of your abilities. When we expect something from someone, we are essentially offering them a chance to harm us. Focus instead on what you think of yourself. Being self-aware implies that we are taking charge and discovering more about ourselves in the process of doing so. Recognize your worth and refuse to tolerate being treated in a manner that is less than you deserve. Change is necessary for yourself. However, do not alter your behaviour for the wrong reasons, such as to please someone or in the expectation that they would like you more. When it comes to relationships, keep in mind that self-worth is essential. No matter how much your partner loves you, if you don't esteem and respect yourself, you will be unable to sense their affection for you.

It's okay to feel,
you are brave enough to heal.

Grief — To deal with losses, each one of us has a unique coping strategy. Because healing is not linear, there is no ideal route. Certain thoughts may be triggering from time to time, but they will slow down. And the pain, anger, and uncertainty will find solutions when you connect with reality, and you accept the situation as it is. It is important to grieve properly, especially when the loss is too personal to you. Trying to ignore your discomfort will only make it worse in the long term.

THE BEGINNING IS NEAR

Some things have to end
for better things to begin.

Feelings — For those suffering from anxiety and depression, I know you're all hurting and fighting your battles in silence, but you'll be in a better place in the long run if you allow yourself to feel instead of repressing your feelings. Only by admitting the suffering can one achieve recovery. While you may be concerned about a variety of issues, you have no influence over them. You're conjuring up unlikely possibilities by stressing and overthinking. I wish you the strength to let go of the things that are causing you pain and pulling you closer to it.

You realise a lot when you
keep your feelings aside
and notice their behaviour.

Perspective — When you dwell on obstacles and tragedies, that is precisely what you'll bring into your life. When you alter your perspective and begin looking for answers and potential possibilities, you are putting out positive vibes that will help bring about an excess of them. When you have the ability to see things from a positive perspective, you become more challenging as a person. Recognizing your struggles and hardship, as well as accepting pain, helps you develop mental resilience to deal with difficulties. Everyone goes through life situations where they have no option but to stay strong and confront them; they may even go through a situation that has totally transformed them for the better. A growth attitude about life yields a whole new way of thinking. When you shift your viewpoint, the same circumstances that might have led to failure before, start serving you well.

Dear self,
you hold
so much pain
and still rise,
I'm proud of you.

Bad days let you grow — At some time throughout the day or night, almost everyone experiences feelings of emptiness or hollowness. Not understanding what it is that is making you unhappy or contributing to your dissatisfaction is frustrating. There may be days when you will lose interest in the activities you used to do, and it is perfectly okay to feel this way. There are joyful and sad times in everyone's life and problems are an unavoidable aspect of our existence. We can't live if we don't have ups and downs. As a result, when things become difficult, we learn how to cope with our issues. Spend your time sensibly and enjoy the beauty of the world around you. Life is to be experienced, fully felt, and cherished as much as possible. In the end, bad days allow you to grow, and your heart will no longer be as heavy as it is now.

It's okay to feel broken,
it's okay to feel empty,
it's okay to feel hurt,
it's okay to feel.

Pain is followed
by the beauty of healing.

Closure — It can be very difficult to move forward when we don't have the kind of closure we want. When there is a sudden split in a relationship with no explanation, it is normal to question why we chose to initially ignore the red flags or what we could have done to prevent the heartbreak, given the pain of loss. When someone has made up their mind that you are not a suitable fit, seeking closure will only add more questions. Our connection to what was or might have been often holds us back, so don't wait or try to convince someone, because you'll waste the best years of your life trying to figure out why you weren't enough. Getting no response is sometimes already an answer. Allow your feelings to be expressed. When you embrace your emotions and accept reality, you will find closure in the form of deserving better.

How other people treat you
is a reflection of who they are
and not what you deserve.

You will never be enough for someone else
if you don't feel complete with yourself first.

Kindness — In a society that is continually driven by greed, it is critical to remain humble and compassionate, but it is also critical not to let your kindness become a sign of weakness by allowing others to take advantage of it. Even though people can be cruel to you sometimes, it's important that you don't lower your standards to match them. Always stay grounded and humble because that's rare and attractive.

She is lost in a world,
quietly healing on her own.

Growth — When you try to run away from your difficulties, you create new problems for yourself and make your life more complicated. When you look for short-term solutions, you will inevitably end up with more pain and a significant breakdown in your journey. Appreciate yourself for how far you've come and be patient with your struggles. Instead of seeing your mistakes as failures, consider them as lessons to be learned and identify what you need to take away from them.

THE BEGINNING IS NEAR

There is beauty
in a love that starts with you.

Acceptance — As you learn and practice self-acceptance, you will be able to naturally embrace others. You will be able to handle difficulties with serenity because you will understand that it is not indicative of your whole existence. We recognise our qualities easily, but when it comes to our flaws and weaknesses, we feel an overpowering feeling of guilt and humiliation. To cultivate acceptance, you must embrace all your undesirable sides, including your emotions, perceptions, and past by being completely honest with who you are. You may be a flawed individual, but you are perfect in your imperfections. You don't have to be anything else but improve your previous self and get better with every phase of your life.

Time is a healer
and you'll bloom
along the way.

Rare soul — Sometimes the pain in your heart breaks you just as you want to heal, and trying to keep yourself occupied all the time can be difficult. Even if you don't deserve the hurt, even if you don't deserve to suffer this much, tell yourself every day that you are strong enough to let go of the things that break you. Situations may be toxic, bringing numbness affecting you all over. Take it one day at a time and develop a list of your favourite activities to do and write down some goals. Erase anything that connects you to your past, which is continuously haunting you, and delete any negative memories that are adding to your suffering. Be patient with growth, healing is a slow and gradual process. So allow yourself time to heal and blossom. This is only another stage in your life, take it as a learning experience and move on. Make a new start, a new beginning, without clinging to the old. Make time to do things that will improve your mental health. You are one-of-a-kind, lovable, and, most importantly, a precious and lovely soul.

Value yourself without feeling guilty about it.

Silence — The silence says so much when someone's not with you anymore. Every moment that makes you think of them, is a reminder of how deeply you two were connected to each other. You know the pain when it gets difficult to breathe, knowing there's no future to it. But slowly in time, you'll make way for healing, you'll fall in love with yourself first, you'll start living for the moments that bring you peace, even if it has to be in the absence of them.

Don't believe yourself to be weak
in order to keep their perception of you.

Love yourself — In a universe where we've been taught to put others' needs ahead of our own, it might be hard to have empathy for our own well-being. You have been through a lot and you're becoming stronger with each passing moment. The practice of loving yourself forces you to take care of your own needs. You will learn to give to yourself, and as a result, you will progress into the person you want to be. The depth of your relationship with yourself and others is the most influential in determining your life experiences. Spend time cultivating your own worth. Being kind to yourself is the most productive thing you can do for your life. If you love yourself, you will enjoy a wonderful sense of well-being and a higher level of reliability. No matter how hard you try, you will never be flawless, but you are perfect just as you are, in your imperfections. And most of all, allow yourself to be completely honest with who you are. Be ready to forgive yourself for whatever mistakes you may have made in the past, and those actions you feel guilty about. Give yourself the love that you deserve.

To be kind
starts with being
gentle with yourself.

Forgiveness — The guilt we hold is often what binds us to the past. It is such a strong emotion that it may emerge in a variety of unpleasant ways. Making peace with the old days and forgiving ourselves for past mistakes is difficult. Everyone struggles with accepting responsibility for their actions, although it is the only way to move on. Self-forgiveness is a kind of love in which you fill your life with compassion and affection by learning from your mistakes. In the long run, these moments of agony, shame and anger will provide you with a better perspective on how to handle people and life circumstances.

The world can wait,
fix yourself first.

A gentle reminder — Love can exist in so many ways, but I hope that you fall in love with yourself before choosing someone else. There is so much to learn when you give time to yourself. Your happiness and peace should never be dependent on someone. There will be many who fail to notice the spark within you, but I hope that you never stop believing in yourself because you are powerful just the way you are.

Your wings hold the strength
to fight your own battles.

Mental resilience — Nothing is more dangerous than a person who has gone through the most difficult moments alone and emerged stronger. This version of them is stronger in many aspects because they have learned to trust their own voice even when everything around them is blurry. They understand how tough the recovery process is. A winding route that demands patience and self-belief. A person like them has no intention of giving up; even if their soul becomes tired, they will continue to push themselves a bit harder on the days that seem dark.

Life teaches you to be strong,
all by yourself.

You are your healer — In truth, you only have yourself to rely on since other people will never fully know what is going on in your head. Some friends will vanish, the people you thought you were in love with will turn their backs on you. Other people may be unable to lessen your suffering because they are unaware of the extent of your pain and the depth of your grief. One thing you will learn is that the only person you can rely on is yourself. It is only you who can help yourself. As a result, it is best to follow your path. When you direct your attention away from pain and to more beautiful areas of your life, you may alter the way your body reacts to the discomfort. You are the one who gets to choose how much energy you want to carry with you throughout the day and consequently throughout your whole life. Take charge of your future and recognize that you are the only one who can bring you where you want to go in life. Because you are your own healer, lover, and a whole damn universe.

Self-love is
when you feel close
to being yourself.

Bravery — Loving yourself is the bravest thing you can do. It takes trust, learning, and feeling to truly care for yourself. It is important to allow yourself to feel everything, no matter how scary or uncomfortable it may seem. You will also make mistakes, but that is okay. Remember that the biggest mistake you can make is not trying at all. It is important to remember that you are worth it, no matter what anyone else may say.

The timing of the universe
has its own magic.

Faith — Life might be difficult even for the kindest of hearts at times but remember that nothing is permanent. It simply takes time and inner strength to cope and grow through it. Keep your peace and your relationships with close friends and family safe. They are the ones that sincerely pray for you on every tough route.

Forgive your heart,
it has fought enough.

Happiness — Focusing on the present moment can help us feel happier and more content. Remembering and reflecting on joyful memories and experiences can lead to positive emotions in the present. Happiness is subjective and can be cultivated, leading to positive outcomes in life. To create happiness for others, we must first change our own outlook on life. Many people believe that obtaining a state of happiness requires being self-aware and to be at peace with yourself. They fail to see that being happy simply involves appreciating each emotion, appreciating the blessing of being able to breathe, and being thankful for each new day. We often tend to overcomplicate things to make our lives more miserable. You must remember that life is a mixture of challenges, grief, pleasure, and happiness; if there was no sadness in life, we would not cherish happiness. If life isn't making you happy, chances are it's because you're not making yourself happy either.

Don't let anyone
dim the light
within you.

Motivation — It might be quite simple to fight at times, but motivation may disappear too quickly, especially when we fall short. Failure is not always a negative thing if you learn from it. However, there is a difference between trying and learning, and giving up as soon as things get difficult or frightening. Your mind is always urging you to quit trying and take a rest. But remember, if you go on despite the voices telling you to stop, you are more likely to succeed. It may be all too simple to focus on the obstacles you face when tackling a large purpose, particularly when dealing with difficult scenarios. It creates uncertainty and weakens your confidence. Instead, since motivation is a temporary emotion, you must always strive to be the greatest at what you do. Instead of focusing on the result, emphasise the process. Your continued tiny efforts, which boost your confidence and reduce stress, are what move you ahead. You have a better chance of achieving your goals over time if you focus on the things you can control and then do what you can to influence them for the better.

We fall only to rise again.

Timing of the universe — Regardless of whether something is good or terrible, it occurs because it serves a purpose. I believe that an endless amount of energy guides us towards what we were supposed to do. You can influence your luck up to a point, but certain circumstances are out of your control. Some people can accept it, while others may feel it is a complete fabrication and every action will eventually come back to haunt them, no matter how good or horrible. It's possible that we don't always have the full view. Maybe if we attempted to see things from a different viewpoint, we would understand that everything that happens to us, no matter how wonderful or horrible we perceive it to be, is truly a part of life. However, it usually takes time, and in some cases, a very long time, to figure out why something happened to us in the first place. It is entirely up to us how we choose to look at things and which option we decide to choose, because nobody has the power to alter things for us.

THE BEGINNING IS NEAR

With patience
you grow, heal and shine.

You are the light — When life moves at a quicker pace, you are left behind, unable to pursue your ambitions. Things are changing so quickly that you begin to feel empty deep inside your heart. You sink in grief and gradually lose yourself. But it's good to pause and appreciate life as it is, to enjoy moments without overthinking them, and to feel what you're going through because there's always a part of you that grows in the dark and deserves to be seen in the light.

It's okay to slow down,
you can always start again.

Hope — It is a fuel that keeps you going. Looking forward to brighter things ahead even when all around you is gloomy. Hope is not the wish for things to be perfect, but the belief that things will become better. You may feel like you are at the pinnacle of failure when you keep trying and don't get the outcomes you want. But when circumstances seem bleak, you are encouraged to learn a lesson that is much more important than you realise. This is when faith comes into play. When we hope, we believe. We have faith in our ability to achieve and see our dreams for a better future fulfilled.

Trust the timing,
everything happens for a reason.

THE BEGINNING IS NEAR

Oh darling,
you keep telling me
about the moon and the stars
when you are the whole
damn universe.

Purpose — The purpose of life is to discover beauty in what you do, and to find pleasure and happiness while you breathe. Its main purpose is to bring serenity and peace into your life and to resonate with you and your soul. Most of us just go through life seeking it either through career or societal achievements but it's not as difficult as it seems. The solutions are all around us, strolling down the street. We are all here for a reason, trying to solve life's mysteries.

Right people — We come across different people, with different energies, and not everyone will stick around. Some will leave us but not without teaching us lessons. When we are experiencing a peak of success, it is likely to attract more people. When we're going through a breakdown the reverse is true. People we think we want to be with may go, while those that really match our vibe and energy, are more likely to stick around through our difficult times. We should appreciate and express our gratitude to everyone who improves our life and makes it more comfortable.

Your soul is
what makes you attractive.

The journey — We're all broken in our own ways, trying to heal from what broke us. The journey may not always be steady but keep moving forward from the things that don't serve you anymore. You belong to a place where you can grow. Allow yourself to confront and learn from the mistakes you made, as well as develop and evolve as a result of those experiences. Pain is not the only emotion that can be felt. There is more to your existence than the struggles you've endured this far in life.

Love is rare,
a paradise of two hearts.

Passion — One of the most heartbreaking parts is that far too many people never discover their passion or are too hesitant to follow it. Career successes are more satisfying and enjoyable when they are driven by passion since it leads to purpose and gives you a clearer path for what you want to accomplish. Your voice should be heard more when choosing a position that you are enthusiastic about. Spend some time figuring out what you are fascinated about. If you are unsure, identify the interests and actions you enjoy that truly make you happy. When you dedicate yourself to what you believe to be your passion, happiness and contentment will follow. Sometimes you must expose yourself to some tough circumstances to discover your passion. While you take the time to engage in some serious introspection, don't let your doubts or worries of failure stand in the way of finding your passion. Find a job that allows you to follow your passions during your free time until you can convert your passion into a career; at that point, you'll transform into the most unstoppable version of yourself.

That risk you are afraid to take
will change your life.

Moments — Many things in life are unexpected. When you put your trust in someone, they may end up betraying you or leaving you feeling devasted. You should be aware of several things: you are everything you could and ought to be. You should have faith in yourself. The focus should ultimately be on you and your life. Love more and hate less because nothing is everlasting. Live your life as you wish and find satisfaction in what you do. Since the present is all we have, live in it.

Life is between
moments and wild dreams.

Time — Healing usually comes in phases. The stronger the connection was, the deeper the wound goes, and it will take longer to recover. Losing a loved one is always difficult, but for most people, time heals the wounds or at least lets them embrace the pain, but the scars remain. The human mind always lingers on memories which make it tough to let go, allow yourself enough time to process your feelings. Nothing and no one can cure your sorrow until you allow them to. It is healthier to live in the present and to accept your past without regret. Whatever occurred is irrevocable, there is no point in spending your time or energy on it and ruining your mental serenity over it.

You deserve to be loved
without having to leave
your flaws in the dark,
away from the light.

Listen — Listen to your heart, it carries your dreams and it will tell you where to go. Trust your intuition, it knows what's best for you. Learn to hear yourself, you already know what you need to do. So go ahead and follow the path that is meant to be yours, it will guide you where you need to be.

THE BEGINNING IS NEAR

She's a healer to the soul,
the healer of the heart,
the truth of pure love,
there is no lie in
the way she exists.

A forever of love still waits for us.

The end — Never let the fire in your heart fade away, even when you are hurt, feel empty, or reach your lowest point in life. You can't change something until you first allow the change to take root within you. There will be days when you'll consider giving up no matter what stage of life you are in right now. Since our society is driven by age, numbers and reputation, the pressure to succeed, and the weight of responsibilities always prevent you to look at life from a better and clear perspective. And thus, you are always searching for the moments that define you for who you want to be and not for who you are. You must remember at this point that you are never too old to start over and that your potential is limitless. And remember not to allow anything to break you because endings are nothing but beginnings. Even in your darkest phase, there's hope because you are still breathing and that's a reason to keep going. The beginning is here.

ABOUT THE AUTHOR

EVENFALL — Prabhu Nair is a writer who trusts in the influence of language and thus utilises it to create an upward spiral of energy and positivity in his readers' lives. He was born and raised in Goa, India, with an intense desire to build the future of his dreams. Over the years he has worked as a content writer for various media sources and well-known publications. He has been seeking solutions to life's mysteries and typically seeks them in books. He has gained prominence for his writings about mental wellbeing, recovery, and positivity using the pen name Evenfall. He has always been optimistic and sees the world differently discovering the exceptional in the ordinary. The majority of his thoughts are derived from everyday experiences and through conversations with his readers.

Scan the code to discover more from Evenfall:

More books from
THE POETICS PUBLISHING

What is Left of Us
Shreya Maurya

Labyrinth Heart
Naiad

Bullets and Silver Linings
Lorelei

Printed in France by Amazon
Brétigny-sur-Orge, FR